The Usher's Torch

Linda Rose Parkes

Hearing Eye

Published by Hearing Eye 2005

Hearing Eye
Box 1, 99 Torriano Avenue
London NW5 2RX, UK
email: hearing_eye@torriano.org
www.torriano.org

Poems © Linda Rose Parkes 2005
ISBN: 1870841 98 0

Acknowledgements

I am grateful to the magazines and anthologies in which the following poems first appeared: *Ambit* for 'In the Beginning was Menses', 'The Curator', 'but today you love me in my silk pyjamas' and 'Thoroughfares', *Leviathan Quarterly* for 'The Punter' and 'Nanny's Coffee', *The Interpreter's House* for 'The Orange Sumac', *Rialto* for 'My Middle Ear', *Magma* for 'The Berlin Cruise Boat' and 'Mama God', *Orbis* for 'In the Gallery of Virgins', *The Keats-Shelley Review* for 'The Distant Aunt', *The National Poetry Anthology* for 'Discovering' and 'The Deer Woman', *writers inc. Anthology* for 'Our Father's Genitals'. Poems have also appeared in *World Poetry* (special issue), *The Dybbuk Of Delight, As Girls Could Boast, Virago New Poets, Reactions 4, Pen&inc.* and *In the Company of Poets* (Hearing Eye).

I would like to acknowledge my tireless friend and critic, Helen Haywood, for the dialogue and inspiration; Katherine Gallagher, for her encouragement and generosity; and Michael Freeman, often the first to see the poems, for sending me back to the drawing board. And I would like to thank my editors, Susan Johns and John Rety. – LRP

This publication has been made possible with
the financial support of Arts Council England

Printed by Catford Print Centre
Designed by Martin Parker at silbercow.co.uk

Contents

For Sylvia, my mother
and Carole, my sister.

The Distant Aunt

She'll ride in from the Ice Mountains,
mists dragging her rough cloth
where she's concealed a purse of coals
to trade for whisky, a tot of milk.
Steam still rising off her pony,
I'll smooth clean sheets for her,
shake out a duvet.

There'll be hammering across the street,
voices and music from a radio
as she stands in the middle of the room
and we converse with signs.
A gesture comes to mean
the laundry, bitter herbs,
desire for chestnuts.

Not everything will be easy:
her toilet habits, her neglecting
to flush; the way she messes up
the towels, shares my jewellery –
and when friends drop in
makes such complicated drinks
(as if it were they who'd trekked miles across snow plains)…

Some days I'll miss the instant foods,

the shelf life of a few minutes;
hours carefully cordoned off
with a rush in between
which keeps things moving.
She has no signs for tired or late.
We wake in a loose expanse of trust,

studded with light and sudden
winds which blast the roof
or spread the pollen.
I start a thought and keep crossing
back for a set of instructions,
a dropped notebook: as if I was
charting a lost self

who'd set off for the mountains
with provisions,
an indelible memory
for maps. Even the crumbs
on the formica, the amber liquid
in the glass, will be fresh events
in an old country.

The Trader's Galleon

One of these days, he'll untangle the wool box,
knots of blue pearl, emerald, black
and moonstone.

But now his fingers ply the yarn
in and out of the pricked canvas
and he finishes the sky:

a bolt of sun shot through a mist
of veils, mewling seabirds
swooping low over the horizon.

Light holds the water
and water holds the light
in a tryst that's seamless.

He gathers the plumes
and shadows to the tide, skeins
the wind into the creaking sails.

The Punter

Let's say I start with sky. A layer of cirrus, some scud
shafted with light. But this isn't about weather
or where I happen to be going when I see this hard-bitten,
sixty-something bloke in his auto, listening to a song on the radio.

This is about how I make him listen, close:
I want a lover with a slow hand. I want a lover with an easy touch.
Get him to say things like: 'I'll give you one anytime, you tart'.
Make him wonder what happened to the old tunes

before I interview his wife and all his lovers to conjure up
a loss, a life passed by: *not come and go in a heated rush.*
No silks, oysters, no talented foreplay, this is about me sifting
an image of rough hands, importunate pricks;

sorry fucks enacted in minutes of waking or falling back
to sleep. At the same time knowing the moment of lift,
the real scoop to fetch sighs, is always, but always, the discovery
of treasure, buried hours of gold showering sparks.

But herein lies the danger: loose a creature in the forest,
you have to track, leave the path, till you're no longer familiar
with the habits of trees, the tread of soil,
when the creature changes

into rarer furs, indigenous to shadow. And even if the bloke
appears to remain seated, once he's spotted the punter,
he does a bunk, stashing the dross along with the gold,
the song almost finished.

Which brings me face to face with my own slim knowledge
of the heart in its electric skin, the spine live with static.
Music of the groin, ecstasy of quim, when they're loved
just right.

The Curator

Yet here I am, gazing through an old window
of a gabled house with intricate glass doors
cased in iron flowers.

On the inside, a set of porcelain galleons
you wouldn't remember. One in particular,
redolent of indigo, moss and ochre.
   Next, the bottles carefully labelled.
Item 1: Memory of Conversation
               outside the Cathedral in Winter.
Item 2: Colour of Your Eyes Remembered
               on Copse Path through Fronds and Mixed Ferns.
Items 3, 4 and 5: Mixed Juices. Flowering Magnolia.
               Hands Travelling between Thigh and Navel.
A series: Spats, tied up in muslin,
               scented with pot-pourri.

But the knowledge of your former heart,
freckles on left breast, bushel of belly,
vagina with its folds of blackness –
I've stowed faithfully
in silent vats.

Every day I walk the great halls,
lyrical, confiding, given over to tears,

sometimes to scorn.

Of all the treasures in the storehouse,

I don't intend to let go

of that galleon. I clean the rigging,

dream of setting sail

one day, in fair winds.

In the Beginning was Menses

Her blankets thrown carelessly back one morning
He was taken off guard, realised
how close to the surface blood was.

Sun scooped the washline of cottons but He felt bewildered:
how to handle the heart always pumping.
And the skin stretched transparent over the raw.

It wasn't exactly what He'd had in mind
with all His careful scrapings, His discrete particles.
Salt molecules, atoms of stars,

all those early mornings and late nights
sieving the air – for qualities of light and photosynthesis –
through an oak-leaf colander.

How had He failed to make allowance for such quantities
of blood? He started to dread spills; didn't have the stomach
for the production of knives, nuclear fission, accidents with harpoons.

Squeamish about bleeding from inside,
He worried a lot about women's menses, the shortness of cycles;
was bothered by smell, the messy tampons

or babies' heads crowning, tearing the tissue.
He hadn't anticipated the way things would leak
and was growing desirous of

odd socks snitched on brambles, millions of trees
blowing; a woman's sheets tugging at pegs,
tangy as lemons and best weather

for running to the top of the hill; lazing all day
flat on His back pretending clouds are horses.

There was much more pain than He'd imagined.

In the Gallery of Virgins

So here I am — smack
                    in the middle of the castle;
fresh-cut roses in right-hand
corner of the room, new queen
stirring, half in sleep
          next to the king...

a nun (yes, tiptoeing towards me)
carrying a glass phial
of blood
which she empties noiselessly
on the dimpled sheet close
                    to the queen's hymen.
Too late to warn of the king's restless eyelid —
whooossh of her cloth, flight back
across the stone hall... (the queen's crown
   now hangs by a fine thread, indeed).

But what sly spoke am I
in the master narrative
(surely not a prayer sent
to redeem the nun's lapsed heart
which the queen had taken in
when she removed the horsehair shirt
with a kiss, a plate of sweet fresh figs)?

                              Ssssh! His lordship *wakes*
as she's climbing back up the stairs,
to where she'll prepare the Gallery of Virgins
for the queen's bloodied sheet.

Ah – and here's the king's falconer
on the far side of the grass,
ready to unleash the hawk
which skirmishes, frets.

Meanwhile, I've morphed
        to Chance Angel,
acting on a whim
to snatch the queen and her nun
            from sovereign retribution.
        Note that slit of light

pushing through the window
onto the bridal drapes
        strewn heavy on the bed.
            That chink
        in the shadows
                beyond the last stair.

Believing Angels

Skimmed by breeze it was a clean start,
winter;
his mind contained
by the light from the Atlantic
as he walked the bay,
believing angels sleep rough on the sea front:
that all vagabonds are angels
who can carry a thought long distance.

Today he was required to be perfect,
because he feared his love was waning.
He took the dangerous route
around the sea-water pool,
waves on either side rubbing,
just enough dry for him to walk

along the slippery ledge
between two vistas,
telling himself
he must be mad.
He couldn't swim well,
not a soul in sight.
Half-way,

he came upon a fish washed up by the tide:
an indeterminate *large and silver*,
with distressed gills, unreadable eyes,
a plea which represented risk,
a destabilising posture

as a wave sucked the beige-shoed
foot closer to the Atlantic,
the near side of the pool fetid
with seaweed, full of rock shadow.
Still no soul in sight, the morning early.

To die now, like this –
one short slide,
a blow to the head
and the thought
didn't end here.
But he wasn't to be found wanting,
though death was as real to him
as his sodden shoes,
yet no more powerful than the fish
which bore all the hallmarks
of an angel, as strange
as the strangeness of his heart.

Deshabillé

A broken bag goes around
on the turnbelt, some of its contents
spilled: a pair of white underpants,
a man's white vest,
a pair of blue underpants
circulating like a bulletin...

This man eats cheap marge,
scrimps on the basics.
And having paid for the fare
at the cost of all else,
somewhere in arrivals
he stands glaring at betrayal.

The truth is...
He's been arrested on landing
at Heathrow, carrying a false
passport and heroin.
No. He's a political refugee –
his luggage was boarded without him.

What really happened is this:
as the stewardess was serving him beer
over Düsseldorf or Helsinki –
he left by the rear door. His coat flying

open he became a bird, spreading his tail
feathers the four corners of the earth.

This is the real truth:
freed at last from down-at-heel gravity,
orbiting naked with Orion,
the man had packed
all his belongings
into this one broken bag.

In the Autonomous Kitchen

But today I side-step out of the rain,
push open the door of
The Dream Kitchen
with its aroma of coffee
and gleaming white cups,
a lemon jug standing in the alcove,
a basket of dried herbs.
      From the moment
I hoist myself onto the high stool
at the counter with the built-in wine rack,
every moment will be of my own making
and all things will turn on a new axis
of slow thought in the autonomous kitchen,
where what I know to be lost
can be redeemed
as I rifle through cupboards
to prepare a feast, lift from the trestle
a few shining pans;
the tea towels, citrus and crisp as the linen
of a brand new dress I wore long ago
on the morning of some uplifting news,
half forgotten but there –
a flickering presence,
like breezes waking a green hem.

The best half hour
is before the kitchen fills
with thirst for tea, someone passing the biscuits –
over the head of what I've stepped out of:
the tedium, the blame, the headlong lies
and joshing (which I keep very close
with my memory repeat button
to remind myself I got away).
This last half hour before the kitchen reels
with chatter and steam and people
I cherish, bursting in
through the door
as if they've always lived here.

Nanny's Coffee

Every young girl crazy with pain
would find solace in Nanny's roomy girth,
the thick aroma of exhortations
to put some blood back in the veins

by drinking *le bon café, noir et sucré*.
Now, if *you* were Antigone,
this coffee might throw the tale
off course, pulling you to the roof

of your mouth, the needy furze
at the back of the tongue.
With coffee warming in the hearth,
you could find yourself starting

to be lulled by the sight of the steam,
the sound of Nanny's voice,
feel of her housecoat pressed
to your cheek. For you, hope never has fled

that far – so far you couldn't call it back
with the thought of a party, a new dress,
the handsome bloke who's bound
to glance your way.

But imagine: the flagstones, winter and cold
cold morning after days without sleep;
your rebel brother rotting on the road and
no one else to bury him against the king's edict.

Our heroine knows she has no choice
but to be entombed with him.
Le sale espoir! This kidding oneself.
And look at Nanny –

all love and anguish as she bellows
the fire, grabs the pot. You can taste
her sweat from where you're sitting
as daybreak filters through the room.

Her roughly swept back hair falls
loose over one eye and she pushes it
roughly behind her ear.
No thoughts but for Antigone;

that stubborn girl will break her heart.
But no – it must not come to that!
Drink, ma petite, come warm yourself!
Let sleep gloss over ugly times. What's done is done.

Looping the Yarn

There's a *click clack click
clack*, hundreds of years
away. A woman knitting
as she wound through the lanes

hurrying to finish a pair
of Jersey hose
in time for the next
Southampton shipment.

Part of her had worked itself
in as she plied the yarn:
grainy heat from her palms,
spores of hair, the underlying

percussion of her heartbeat
seeped into the raw fibre
with salt-blue particles
of the thrumming tide.

As the hose were eased
onto Queen Mary's feet
softly past the cleft
of her ankles

a murmur of sheep
  strayed through the window
    from flocks grazing
      on the banks of the Nene.

And the hills unravelling
  frost and steep
    shadows broken
      by luminous spills

of green breathed
  the light of the dawn
    the hour the stitches
      were cast on.

And the wind which shook
  the tips of the grasses
    flickered the walls
      of the castle keep

was the wind fomenting
  the mouth of the estuary
    billowing the sails
      of laden ships.

As the hose were unfurled
  over Mary's calves, gently, gently

up her wan thighs, and then fixed
with a *payre of greene silke garters*

and as she leaned her neck
across the block and
blood splashed her white hose
filled her shoes of *Spanishe leather*

there was the *click*
of a stranger hundreds of miles
away, looping the yarn over
and under. *Clack.*

Intruder

Don't you ever tire of fright,
long to make light bounce at the door?
It's not easy to make dark hang back
in service to the good dream:
you have to learn to orchestrate.
Try offering him a gin and orange,
sit him in a chair under the moon
with an endless sigh of silk cushions.
He turns out to be ill-fated, young,
has left his life's work in the boot
and can't remember where he's left the car
in a warren the size of the Atlantic.
Don't let the glass shake or he'll leave
before we have the chance to finish the story
which we'll call from now on:
A Fable On The Production Of Light.
It's well past midnight
when he triggers the sensors.
You've been waiting a long time
for the rasp of the door, lain there
listening, bracing yourself
to slip from your bed onto the landing,
trying to haul out your voice.
Slow motion, text-book stuff:
you still fumbling for the switch
knowing he's climbed the first stair.

Forfeit

Your remaining knight whispers:
one day he'd like to fall in love,
sip tall beer under the stars, watch the sun rise
with that someone when branches reach
into the wind and rooks are flying
to the rook house, come to hold parliament
in trees, amble in the spidery grass.
About to close his fingers on your Queen,
the Chess Master leans across the squares.
What exactly does the loser forfeit?

Mornings, when light swims
to the roofs and you stand for minutes
at the window, held by crocuses and frost?
Sex, its slow breeze patterns,
the shadow that falls across the path
between the drainpipe and the blackberry bushes?
Saturday night's piss up?
You can let that go.
Your flat screen
or your new windows,
your sandwich
or your good coat?
The woodlands,
the hills,

the oceans,
the last bus
crashing its gears down familiar streets?

You try to divine the opponent's mood,
embrace the strategies, have one of your own
and two up your sleeve, a triumphal plot.
But the souls of the rooks have already nested.
High over the board their wings beat
and the black knight gallops
to the shoreline:
beads of water hang in his mane,
a curtain of surf blows around him.
One forward, two sideways,
one sideways,
two back.

Wittgenstein's Rabbit

She considered changing places
with the birds. Her ears for their wings,
a straight exchange, she reckoned.
Her furred white stomach for
their speckled breasts.
Beaks, yes, beaks, she'd get the hang of
those funny pecking things
if they could get the hang of teeth.
Their legs and claws, poor exchange,
of course, for the feet well documented
and much loved.

But to trade her voice for the birds'
pandemonium, the feckless warble
they cared to call *song*:
all those frills and trills and fancy
hat tricks to pull the crowds....
She defied all living souls to name
the sounds she made, the exultation
of the discus thrower, the radar ping
of bats, approximating planets
in orbit at low frequence, purring neurons.
Yes, scent came into it too,
a valley of bluebells minutes before dawn,
the grass bejewelled with sleeping pearls.

The enigma of the rabbit aria,
the rabbit poems, their ghostly tunes
like wind sucked off oceans
and echoed through rainbow shells,
the gravity waves of a supernova,
low moan in the dark of the last elm.

The Deer Woman

after David Lynch

When Alvin encounters her
on the road, she's just run over
her thirtieth deer and is crying out
across the ravaged plains
where the gentle beasts spring
out of nowhere.

Will he lay his hand on her sleeve,
boil a kettle he takes from his trailer?
And as he hands her the strong, sweet tea,
offer a tale or rumination to summon
the genius of solace, bring an end
to the deathfest stalking her trail
although she blows her horn
along that stretch of tarmac,
slows right down?

And at that moment as she drives out of view,
does she sense the fragile and sinuous
connections which sometimes
take the shape of a deer
listening at the shadowy edge?
And that for every collision in the landscape,
every dislocation and burden of grief,

there's a magic property in words
which can tilt the earth
in just such a way that man, woman,
deer may let the other pass like tremors
of light, breaking through the surface.

But he looks around him
at the drained fields, where a single tree
stands blasted of leaves,
can find no sense to string
an honest meaning.
Under the stars that night
he barbecues succulent deer
in its crisp juice. And the silence
pours unction on his soul:
the woman continues
as a magnet to the creatures
who fall under her wheels
like figments of an impossible language.

Shadows in the Hall

Voices padding up and down
tea on the brew, smoky flowers.
But there's always a rustle of dark outside
waves bridling with a touch of static
when I make for the door.
And if I'm the last, I hover
at switches, cast my mind about
the room littered with glasses
the chairs still warm.
Each sortie prompts
an icy spasm, a volatile future
between stations
where the land grows eerie
drowned in shadow;
I swim with my arms outstretched
between breakers.

Of course, I haven't gone that far
only a few paces
down the hall
before I bundle myself in
from the nip of cold.

Blood Test

There we were, sat on the edge
of the bed, the doctor pushing up his sleeve,
rubbing salve into his five-year-old arm
before she fed in the needle.
In a straw hat with silk flowers,
I was breathing calm for him;
he summoning courage
like a thousand birds flocking
before an electric storm;
his focus as far as it could travel
from the sluggish trickle
into the plastic tube.

He already knew the terrors
of the flesh: the bath tap
that had winded him below the kidney;
the tight, snipped foreskin
tampered and bruised as we'd eased it
daily down the livid shaft.

And suddenly *Mummy* had to lie down,
take off her hat, loosen her dress –
the straw hat tumbling to the floor.
And as if he'd known since he was

out of nappies, he took hold of my hand;
with his other, stroked rhythmically
across my forehead, memory moving
through his fingers he widened the arc
towards the roots of my hair,
where he spread and softly closed
the circle, his hand sweeping back
above the line of brow, tracing
the route along a secret imprint,
while I lay there, adrift,
the bottle filling with his velvet.

Journey to the Nought

The night is crowded with prayer
  and we're lost between prayer routes.
Even our breathing frets the trees
    along the western horizon
where tonight's sleep
        is tomorrow's
              parting,
eight hundred miles
      to your father's hemisphere.

          I'd go to you out there,
            tell you
                  nothing can come
          between us,
      from end of summer
        to short light of winter.

          But I'm afraid to disturb
                your calculations –
    the number of weeks multiplied
        by minutes – the shape
      of hours in the stars' constellations.

          Each day a subtraction
          from the journey to the nought.

Single Frame

She sits "just for a moment till father gets home."
I count the buttons, chase the stitches;
the colour of my mother's cardigan
is rose granite in the early evening
when sun washes deep inside the stone.
    Nixon smirking on the telly,
she sips her tea. Through the open curtains
dusk bathes the grass; beneath the sill
a stack of records: Mario Lanza, Joan Hammond
whose plush cleavage, full red lips, turn
    my attention back towards my mother,
who each time I look grows more ephemeral
in her cardigan with the crocheted stitch,
the lavender tinge of Yardley's talcum
breathing from her pores.
    The me tucked inside her arm is a freckled
blur against the backdrop as I struggle
to make out what age I was or whether
I was there at all with the full-blown
roses swaying in the rug.
    Yet this image which pushes to the surface
at three in the morning when I'm trying
to sleep, fetches in me what I think
I knew then, at the moment
I first understood it.

I see how the wool chafes my mother's skin,
her breasts are dwindling
beneath the buttons, while her collar bone,
a bleached necklace, is papery-thin,
brittle with longing.
I can hear a language stalled in her blood
like dust and air and spools
of dark crowding the lens
with the loose-covered chairs,
the polished coal bucket.
              The room flies apart
reassembles
        brighter now
around the edges
as if the touchpaper's about to catch.

The Cabin

When everymother went to hospital
it was as if everyfather
had donned a pinny
and was melting oil in a big black pan,
keeping the food hot on the ring
for his daughters to come home
and wash their hands
before the small round steak
could be carefully chewed
with creamy mash.

He was in a good mood,
almost in love
that night he took us
to our first film and saw us
walk the carpeted aisles,
demurely following
the usher's torch
to have Charlie Chaplin
tune our roughly polished
horse-play with a cooked shoe,
a swaying cabin.

We understood about the cabin:
how when everymother

and everyfather were there together,
the world would tilt and we'd go
sliding, holding to cereal spoons
and doorknobs,
holding to table legs
and cushions,
when somebody, crossing
the room too quickly,
upended the house.

Our Father's Genitals

Two china geese on the tiled wall
flying to somewhere like far off Ottawa
or one of the Great Lakes of skittering
reeds where a hand would pass like shade
over the surface. A good sort of hand
for ruffling a wing, like the hand of our
father in gentler mood, plenty of hot water
and a glass of sherry. Him lying there,
soothed inside himself; the pine's silt
needles scratching the window.
My sister and me perched on the bath,
stealing glances. Such a pale sort
of thing, full of secrets.
Surely it wanted to tell us something
in a voice that was beckoning
under the water with whispers around it.
I imagined a wily song, an ocean
of living things, pulled by currents,
remembering tides.
To think it had held one half of us
suspended like geese in mid-flight;
we might never have arrived in our blue
feathers: imagine us frozen there –

the place of shadows we had to cross
to be scooped up, wrapped in our mother.
Tentacle, sacks and limpid spine,
water lapping the rough hairs.

Discovering

They filter through somehow, the old taboos,
though my mother never said
it's dirty
or *you'll go blind*.

But my daughter can't sleep,
buries her head in the pillow, cries.
Eleven p.m., it's too bad to tell.

With hugs I ease it into the light,
assure her it's natural.
I'm forty, she's nine;
I don't say how long it took
for me to love myself.

She clings to me, I stroke her arm;
she has breasts like voles, pubic hair.
Hovers at mirrors, uses passionfruit
on her skin. Wants to be sylph-like,
princessy, not tall, strong;
this need between her thighs.

Again I tell her she is beautiful.
She smells of soil, gorse and peat,
of a bird flying over fields.
She smells of the warm
in the crook of its wings.

Mama God

Impossible now to gather her up, snatch her from fire,
bear her above water in the old way.

Her breasts almost level with mine, my pelvis straining
in the race, I can still hold her, rise up in rage

and indignation; at the least sign of disappointment,
threat, conjure the healing words.

My buttocks poised one inch higher than hers,
I plait her hair, make her eat muesli.

Five years ago I sleep-walked to her bed
to have her coax me out of a bad dream.

At six she saw her father cry, knew how to rock him.
Already hostage to the Mama God,

she knew when he went on crying,
how to cradle.

Marcel Drowning

We knew he was a demon
with a spade, kept his own hens
had nine children.
Once he told us of his near
drowning where currents sweep
you all the way to France
and how his life had passed before him.

I could see his hens spinning
around his head, beating the water
with their wings, feathers
like a pillow shaken loose
drifting up into tangled air
or straggled in the uproar of clucking,
feeder and corn-pail
going down.

The children were stretching out their arms,
the little ones bawling,
the oldest embarrassed by his father's antics:
the threshing and swallowing
of water the way he'd told them
they must never do.

His giant wife as well —
about to jump in

and save him
just as soon as she'd finished
the hundred and one things.

I was nine and I knew the word *semen*.
And most importantly –
his *semen* was there.
Shoals of fish-tailed spermatozoa
darting through the blue tunnels
diving in salt and spume and feathers.

This is what saved him in the end –
his battery of un-hatched children,
the buoyant host of wondrous swimmers.

The Bell Margin

If I start with the feel of the coarse
blanket pulled up to my chin,
the sickness and the slow crossing,

it will lead me back to the Costa Brava
of Franco's Spain: motor-bike police
patrolling the borders,

my father warning us to sit
hushed in the car.
I know nothing yet

about the gold and silver
of the Conquistadores,
Cervantes at the Battle of Lepanto,

the Inquisition, the feudal grandees,
about Carmen or Lorca's Sonnets
of Dark Love.

My mother has bought us a tambourine
with the face of a red bull
and eight tiny bells.

We're ambling along a tall beach
when a crowd jostles...

a jellyfish is staked in the sand –
they're pelting it with stones.

The tent of its flesh is like gently
poached egg whites,
stirred with a drop of cochineal.

But I'm four years old and have no words
when I try to conjure up the sting cells,
terror for the thing that's dying.

An invertebrate language floats
to the surface, the delicate tint
of a wide bell, tentacles dangling;

if I make my way back behind
the child's eyes, what swims
in my head is viscous silence.

My Middle Ear

I possessed one word.
Others will tell of tapestries,
paintings, the Gothic Cathedral
of St. Gatien, but I remember
melon with the picnic:
how I said my first *merci*
at the spot where Mantel
quashed the Moorish conquest
and I was strickened with bad
earache from the clamour
and din, the whinnying horses.

The word was tall
enough to hold
the window,
the shutters
and the smell of baking,
steeped in tobacco,
wafting from the street.

Wide enough to contain
the wardrobe,
the thousands of petals
in the wallpaper,
the basin

and the half-filled water-jug,
my parents eating
downstairs.

It hung upside down
from the bed-head,
swung back and
forth across the ceiling
when I tried to retrieve
it for the waiter
who brought peas
and mashed potatoes
and called me
ma'moiselle.

The Teacup

And every morning, my mother pours
the tea to just below the rim of the thatch.

First to be swallowed by the tide
are the boy in corduroy leggings
and his little terrier watching
for a sign from the boy saying
off to the woods.

Next, the woman in the lace bonnet
who's filled her apron with fresh-laid
eggs and is chatting to the boy
not far from the hen coop where the noisy
speckled hens scratch for seed.

The hills brim and
spill around their heads: the woman
struggles in her tea-logged skirts to hold
the eggs, the boy tries to whistle
his dog and the muffled hens squawk.

I drain the valley in hurried sips,
short, now longer as the tea cools:
out of the swirling contours
of the flood, the bonnet emerges,
the hens, the eggs…

Every morning, I perform this rite
to comfort in his sorrow the great god Pan
who wanders the hills beyond
the cup, calls from the meadows,
through the trees.

Two last gulps and I save the boy
so he can race his dog to the bluebell woods.

Bleat

She called the girl Bleat,
chewed the cud of her hair
which smelled of mating juice.
They'd go out walking,
She-Goat and her lovely companion,
in the world with Sky and thick-scented
gusts of Trees, shrill and pinned back,
scratching the Wind or fanned
with Birds rising,
floating down.
She was filled by these journeyings at night
when Bleat sang wild words as though
she was calling a long way off,
her voice like satin between Stars
and inked around the Moon.

The girl's mother worried.
Apart from She-Goat
with her game of butts —
rearing on hind legs to signal start,
teats tight with the good milk
they couldn't drink, so pungent was it —
who did her daughter love?

On cold days She-Goat loosed her stake
and sauntered home, nibbling
the succulent fibres of the fence.
Bleat sometimes came to her to cry –
nestling into the coarse, muscled neck.

Not that She-Goat worried about Bleat.
She rasped with her tongue
and licked Bleat's salt,
called her name a few times.

Running Without Susan

Two loose-limbed older lads
    slinking across the needled floor,
offering to lift us to the branches.
You and I shaking down cones,
sun splashing in patches
on the ground, mottling our legs.
        Those moments
before our friendship changes –
sap is sticky on the pines, light soaks
the edges of the earth like water.

'*No? Go on…!*'
I think they tried to lift us both –
in a tussle loaded against play –
    then pinned you
(the pretty blonde one) down
and yanked my arm.
    Next thing, one of them's
rucking up your skirt, forcing his hands –
telling me to scram.
Your hair is still in place
from the morning, from the silver brush.

And then I'm running
down the bank,

                         away
down the field.
        Of course I was going
to fetch help; of course, raise
the alarm.
        But suddenly
they'd chickened out – and
Susan, you were running with me...

Yet. How to forgive dissolves
of the self, tinderbox of nil
courage? Where the bird
of the momentous heart
unfolding in the pitched shadows?
Where the coursing
through the air on light,
swallowing the chilled forest?

        And so it is I search for you
now, imagining a nobler film:
buffeted, windswept, a cool angel,
    I scratch, kick, lash out,
        fly into the dark to save you.
Even if they mean to snap
both arms, I won't be running
without you.

Snorkelling in the Red Sea
with my Sister

It takes me ages to fix my mask
and snorkel. You're busy
with your £10 underwater camera,
trying to get a shot of the Lion Fish,
the Emperor Angel.

It distracts you that I stick so close
as if I was only eight
and you had my bus ticket.

Imagine staying down here
with the pulsating sea urchins,
the delicate brain coral.
You, the Masked Butterfly
with lots of yellow;
me, the cubic-headed
Picasso Trigger Fish.

We could swim to Jordan,
Egypt, without passports,
visit the souls of Pharoah's horses,
leisurely now, thumb-size
in their movements.

Find that narrow path
of parted water –
the Jewish half of ourselves
coming towards us.

Homeland

After long security delays
and flooding,
the coach edged past rubble,
deserted tanks, every stark
ledge illumined in the head-lamps.

The coloured lights of Aqaba
reminded me of my native coastline,
but my ignorance confounded me:
Jordan on the left,
Egypt on the right,
a book on Israel,
a Hebrew phrase-book,
the few salty herrings of my grandma's Yiddish.

I knew my mother wished
she'd made her home here,
away from the taboos of
the anglo-smart set
though still recoiling from
the stale breath
of un-brushed Sabbath teeth.

It soothed her
to hear these local entertainers
crooning Frank Sinatra
and Alma Cogan
under fairy-lit date palms.

The Staghorn Sumac

I turn back the way we've come
down the path of buddleia and hawthorn,
air red around the edges
of mid October.
            The next time
I see my son, his voice might be breaking,
tell-tale signs dusting his upper lip
like a plume of woodsmoke blowing
over the rowans.
            When I get to the orange sumac
I stop, examine the fruiting heads,
wishing I'd brought him here,
drawn his hand along the bark's pelt
towards the silence of animal
standing stock-still:
body quivering, senses livened
by the fermentation of leaves.
The furred sweat of rabbits
flashes into the undergrowth
of coppers and cracked greens,
the sticky sap of pine.
            A stag's heart beats
across the forest.

Samuel's Confirmation

Last Friday we celebrated Sabbath,
kipa perched on his head,
short of a kirbigrip.
Now he's sitting across the aisle
with his classmates,
and the jumper I've bought him
is two sizes too big.
He's bathed and washed his hair,
his shoes have been polished.

In front of me is a statue
of the Virgin Mary.
I wonder what she felt,
when she found him in the Temple...
Did you not know I was
in the House of my Father?

Soon the priest's fingers
will draw the sign of the cross
on my son's forehead
where I've planted kisses.
Tip the jug:

Im Namen des Vaters,
des Sohnes und des heiligen Geistes.

And Samuel looks toward me now,
for the reassurance
of his mother's blessing.

She was very, very

The art lay in hesitation. I piled very upon very
in front of *beautiful* – in a string of delays,

flocked them about her on her way to the ball,
a thrall of commas at the great oak doors,

a trajectory to save her from completion.
Tiny, starred explosions vanquishing death,

death as in: end to sparrows circling her
and flying up. Death as in: the prince has scaled

the walls of devotion and sauntered off.
The Palace swooned with incantation, her hair

spun from moonbeams, her cortege the flocks of
nightingales, sparrows, fluttering, singing.

Her veil would be sundered in a burst of stardust
once the Prince had kissed her. After the build-up,

a kiss was a once only, dancing attendance
on the full-stop. I couldn't imagine the fondling of breasts,

the hand up a skirt, the kiss which makes you proud
and lovely, or sticky and dulled.

I still can't imagine how to fall into the kiss
and keep on falling, forever and ever and

Lewd Moll
Sways on the Streets
of Cologne

I'm drunk on them, could ride my shadow
  bare-back to the hill-blown chords of their sampañas,
Cinchona voices drowning the grey streets.

I want to trade my coat for a bright woven poncho.
  Take them home, feed them solid German bread,
sup them on beer at the table of my stories.

I want to pinch and pat, unplait their hair, slide
  my comb through the black, fondle each strand
before I help them undress, tuck them in bed. My bed.

They make me feel naughty.
  I want to dance my umbrella to their bums,
tease and goad to the rhythms of their clackers,

tense their thighs with the knowledge that I almost
  dare myself to touch them there – play the greenest notes,
the hot, sweet climate.

We start here

I love the way your chest hollows under your dressing-gown,
the hair like grass on still dunes.

How when you look at me there's a dance brewing
as if Ry Cooder's on the terrace in a white suit and black shirt.

That time I slipped on the wet tiles – you came running,
your heart on the verge of a kaleidoscope storm… But what if

I asked you, three times a day, to shake off sloth, plump up the
interior, roll back the carpet to the hills, to the river's hidden currents?

Or if I said *put your hand on the beginning of the world
and I'll put mine on the seat of contradictions*

when you're drinking coffee from your yellow cup? Your cigarette
papers on the cloth, your red lighter, behind you a vase of white lilies.

Little by little and all at once, we fold back the skin,
show how to travel.

If I could say *here and here and here* is where your tongue
should hover, your thoughts glide to the edge

as if we were star gazing, as if we were trying to judge
the distance of a leap

between planets…
a good place to start would be the table with the cups, the lilies.

... twirl ...

Let's imagine how the neighbours see us,
framed by a bed lamp through the open curtains.

Pearl, in sequins and red lycra, hovering
on her way to the bathroom, props her weight
on one arm against the wall, watches,
pondering the chances of profit.
  Her lodger, folding away his clothes,
pauses as he glimpses a movement;
on just such a night love might return, glancing
off time in a whiff of perfume.
  And the couple bickering in the house next door
are suddenly caught up in lighter air blowing
into the town and this particular road
                        where, book in hand,
I'm laughing in my sheets while you're threading
your arms through my white gown, taken off
its hook on the door; now you're tying a loose bow,
your greying chest peeping through lace borders…

          and a cotton breeze plays
              between us as you follow
          the crease of other dances
                  in the floating
              interior of a twirl …

gliding, spinning the scope of carpet,
    still wearing your socks,
      you sway from the hip
  and the gown
      falls open.

Contiguity

On the roof of a twelve storey block of flats
he was counting nesting gulls through binoculars.

He could span four miles over a few
breezy trees, a pulse of cars snaking the town.

Clouds drifted, he trained his sights.
And as if by electrical charge or magnet

she entered his field.
Ashamed of advantage but compelled,

he contemplated the lift of stride, tempo.
Scanned her face, eyes… knew the squalls already

and the kisses. Sang his praises to the Mother of
Overlap for this chance to watch her,

oblivious to his gaze, self-contained,
progressing through a crowd.

It was as if he was seeing for the first time
the way she moved inside the world, propelled

by some enormous heat which was also his own:
this radiance punctuated with gulls.

The Laundry Basket

A virtuous woman has a repugnance
to excessive luxury in her underclothing.

La Baronne Staffe *La Maîtresse de Maison* 1892

He takes them one by one
from the basket: cami-knickers
in rose and peach silk, plissé frills,
a comfortable v-seam, birds
and flowers embroidered on lawn
(if ever she's knocked down
by foes and villains
or snared by traffic,
she'll be wearing panties delicate
as cobwebs).
Short of a pleat, a touch of goffering,
this is Mrs. Bauer's frothy trousseau
or the Lucile confection
of chiffon and lace.

He notes the odd hole,
torn gusset,
shakes out each pair,
drapes them on the clothes line –
a rustle of black silk

snags in his hand
as if memory
has woken in the fabric:
the supple art of neat stitching
and electric threads
of courtesans and dancers,
flare in the lightning cloth...

He straightens
bends
reaches deeper in the basket.

Ferret

This morning a woman's singing.
Her voice is out there with the birds
drawing a thin arc from tree to sky.

Dustmen are striking, litter spills
out of the black bags while gulls
take their pickings.

She's dressed, up early, hanging the wash.
Thrushes flitter in the holly
her old man's upstairs sleeping,

the kitchen half in light
half shadow, sliced white bread turning
gold in the toaster, about to be spread

and Dennis the ferret running to meet her
through the echoing pipes she's laid in the garden.
She hears him now, he can smell food.

More than the man sometimes, she loves the ferret
razor-sharp, close to the ground.
And in spite of the dustbins

fouling the air
suddenly she finds herself singing
in the slow wheel of sun.

And yes, sometimes it's true. Instead of an image
of the man (good for nothing lately, other than sleep)
she carries in her heart the hunger of the ferret.

But today you love me
in my silk pyjamas

This is the morning the rain stops
out on the strand, thoughts roll
like a wave combed by salt wind,
we fish with our hands, dance on water.
Tomorrow a ship could dock an army,
a vessel in the brain explode
through the open door where we fall
out of good time.
    But today you love me
in my silk pyjamas, your capacious
heart soothed by the long climb
of buttons that start at the dip of cleavage
into two tipped wings.
      And if you asked me to describe
the soul, I'd say it's a shack
with an old rain barrel where leaves
collect, five goats grazing on the hill
and a neighbour playing Placido Domingo
with Barbara Streisand crescendoing
away bad nerves and loneliness
in the trailer of an immortal film.
        An unerring feel
for the slow now
grows in the light between chair

and table, between the laid-out cups.
I'm alone at the window held by the shadows
stretching this way and that,
finding a moment to take stock,
                    when the neighbour winds
the tape back
three times.

Thoroughfares

Every day I try to protect you
from four-wheel drives,
testosterone junkies
cutting through crossings,
nipping the kerb —
the kind of thing that makes you oh so fierce.
I want to shut my eyes
and let the moment pass
so we can saunter on, hand in hand,
pretending the world loves a pedestrian
and life resides in gentle pavements.

We don't pretend, of course,
and I don't save you.
Intake of breath, the cold rush,
no gentle pat, no *there, there*.
This is fight unto the death:
your anger versus shit-load
of metal at forty miles an hour
down a narrow road and *man
do I look cool to the peasants
in my Porsche Carrera.
Who gives a fuck.*

Well, actually, you do,
and you're about

to show them,
like Wyatt Earp and Emily Davison.
But what about me?
I'm kneeling beside your broken body,
your blood spilled onto my sleeves, my breasts.
I won't tell you it wasn't worth it –
there isn't time for that and anyway,
who knows what could change the world?

No. Come back, is what I say:
each journey slow enough I promise -
always on foot, without leaving
the country, the light we breathe.
Whispering now into your hair,
into the furrows on your neck,
into your hands, behind your knees.
Whispering in the dark we touch.
I'm leaning closer to your eyes,
to the creases of your mouth,
your belly; I press the kiss
of long, slow thoroughfares.

Grey Mare

In this age of sanitised
malnourished
young,
how I love you to extol
the virtues of unhygienic
older women.
Wrapped in your dressing-gown,
unwashed, unkempt,
I feel *pleased*
with myself, for having gone
the distance after all these years,
to find myself full of allowance
and forgiveness.
So when you say
Toots, would you pass me the milk?
call me your old grey mare
and pat my rump should I happen
to lag (only because I dream,
not because my legs can't carry me
colt-speed up La Grande Rue),
I feel affectionate towards
myself, see an honest haunch,
a coat of sheen, the glorious
wild and matted mane

of my own sheer horse-power,
my enormous will
which keeps me moving
onwards, onwards.

The Hedgehog Cake

The hedgehog cake is a success,
prickled perfect on the plate
of knife-edge furies.

She says how they plan to stay
together for the children's sake,
here with industrial empire homes
complete with guards.

She misses the copse,
the low lying branches of oaks.

Smoothing oil on her skin,
she mourns the body storing fat,
tells me how she menstruates
for weeks.

What can I say?
I who took another route.

As we kiss goodbye,
she's determined to be calm.

My most successful cake so far,
she waves and laughs.
Two red smarties for eyes.

The Berlin Cruise Boat

Mulling over the usual defeats,
I'm traipsing past the Oxo Tower
when strains of Die Moldau spill over
the Thames with lights from the dining saloon:
grand piano, cello, violins…
Welcome, my friends who sail the waterways,
wie geht es Ihnen?
White tables, cups in *Zwiebelmüster*,
jewellery and smart dresses.
Ah, how quickly I'm losing my few words
of German – I've never even seen the Elbe
or the Brandenburger Tor, chariots flying.
Now chairs scrape, people moving
to the dance-floor as a waltz strikes up,
building to a seamless glide behind glass.
And there's Herr Müllemann, his coat tails flying!
Dancing like a man in good health:
Eleonore, listening closely to the music
and Dieter, half-way through a ciggy…
wonder if he still listens to Tom Waits?
Even my ex is here and smiling, off the booze
he's found new love.
The saloon is filling with faces of passengers
and in their midst I can see me,
a woman lit with the genius of language,

laughing, speaking fluent German
in a life I've abandoned. She turns to me, waves.
And again the orchestra's starting up, trailing
a slow lead-in on violins.
I navigate the half-crossed, half-dismantled
borders and as the boat slides away, the thought
flows past: nothing is ever really lost, no hope,
no effort of love, left off or broken,
which can't be rescued in the secret currents;
party streamers, lights flaring, or just a gentle piece
of music. We continue to arrive.

A Dream of Ransom

The next minute
you've been kidnapped.

I've no idea who's taken you.
Your voice comes down

a tunnel without light
telling me I have no
bargaining power:

I cannot pay
with love.

Your voice is calm
and sensible.

Love
never saved
anybody.